La Salle

and the Exploration of the Mississippi

Explorers of New Worlds

La Salle

and the Exploration of the Mississippi

Daniel E. Harmon

Chelsea House Publishers
Philadelphia

Prepared for Chelsea House Publishers by:
OTTN Publishing, Stockton, N.J.

CHELSEA HOUSE PUBLISHERS
Production Manager: Pamela Loos
Art Director: Sara Davis
Director of Photography: Judy L. Hasday
Managing Editor: James D. Gallagher
Senior Production Editor: J. Christopher Higgins
Series Designer: Keith Trego
Cover Design: Forman Group

First Printing
1 3 5 7 9 8 6 4 2

Library of Congress Cataloging-in-Publication Data

Harmon, Daniel E.
   La Salle and the exploration of the Mississippi /
   Daniel E. Harmon.
       p.   cm. – (Explorers of new worlds)
Includes bibliographical references and index.
ISBN 0-7910-5952-9 (hc) – ISBN 0-7910-6162-0 (pbk.)
1. La Salle, Robert Cavelier, sieur de, 1643-1687–
Juvenile literature. 2. Explorers–Mississippi River
Valley–Biography–Juvenile literature. 3. Explorers–
France–Biography–Juvenile literature. 4. Mississippi
River Valley–Discovery and exploration–French–
Juvenile literature. 5. Mississippi River Valley–History
to 1803–Juvenile literature. [1. La Salle, Robert Caveli-
er, sieur de, 1643-1687. 2. Explorers. 3. Mississippi
River–Discovery and exploration.] I. Title. II. Series.

F352.H28 2000
917.704'1'092–dc21
[B]   00-043074

Contents

A Boundless
New Land

La Salle claims the Mississippi River basin for France in April 1682. He named this enormous region Louisiana, after King Louis XIV of France.

I

On April 9, 1682, the French explorer René-Robert Cavelier, Sieur de La Salle, planted the French flag near the mouth of the Mississippi River. He and his men—30 French soldiers and about 100 Native American guides—had spent two months following the mighty river's course in canoes. They had started in the **Great Lakes** far to the north and had paddled all the way to where the river empties into the Gulf of Mexico.

In a small ceremony, attended only by his men and perhaps a few curious Native Americans, La Salle claimed the entire Mississippi River basin—the land drained by the river system—for France. In honor of the French king, Louis XIV, he named this vast region **Louisiana**. After planting the French flag, La Salle's men raised a cross and chanted prayers in Latin. They then made their claim legal—in the eyes of Europeans, at least—by signing a document drawn up on the spot by one Jacques de la Metairie, a **notary** from Fort Frontenac who had made the journey with them. The Indians who had lived on the land for generations were never asked their opinions.

Although the news of La Salle's claim would not reach Europe for months, those at the ceremony knew this was a glorious day in French history. He had secured a huge area of the new continent of North America for his country. This would give France an edge over her rivals, Spain and England. All three countries were trying to exploit the new continent's resources: gold, furs, timber, and other valuable items. La Salle's voyage of exploration had put France in control of the American frontier.

René-Robert Cavelier was born on November 22, 1643. His family home was located near Rouen,

France, on the River Seine about 70 miles northwest of Paris, the French capital.

The young boy was sent to a *Jesuit* school. The Jesuits are a society of Catholic priests that work

> **"Sieur de La Salle" means "gentleman from La Salle." His family was rich, and La Salle was the name of their estate.**

as teachers and *missionaries*. Their school provided La Salle with a good education. He was especially interested in math and science.

As a teenager, La Salle was fascinated by what he was hearing about lands across the sea. New France was the name given to an area being explored and settled along the St. Lawrence River and the Great Lakes. La Salle's heroes were French explorers like Samuel de Champlain.

Robert's older brother Jean was a missionary in New France. Robert was determined that one day he, too, would see the New World. In the meantime, he studied *navigation*, astronomy, and geography– subjects that would serve him well in the future.

While in his early 20s, Robert asked the Jesuits in Rouen to let him become a missionary like his brother. But the Jesuits said he would not be ready for several years.

Robert could not wait. In 1667 (some accounts record 1666) he left the Jesuits and boarded a ship bound for the St. Lawrence River across the sea. He would arrive in New France not as a missionary but as an adventurer.

* * * *

The French were not the first explorers in the New World. Down the eastern coast, English and Spanish pioneers were building colonies and pushing the frontier toward the west.

The Spanish explorer Hernando de Soto, marching from the south, had led an expedition into the heart of North America in 1541, a century before La Salle was born. De Soto had discovered the vast Mississippi River. But by the mid-1600s, the waterway still remained largely unknown to Europeans.

The French, meanwhile, were exploring far to the north in what is today southeastern Canada. They had arrived in what now is Nova Scotia as early as 1504—only a few years after Columbus had landed in the West Indies. These first French voyagers were fishermen. The French explorers who followed

The name *Canada* comes from a Native American word, "kanata," meaning "village."

From 1539 to 1542, the Spaniard Hernando de Soto and his men explored Florida and much of the American South. He became the first European to see the waters of the Mississippi River.

them were hoping to find a passage through the American continent to the Pacific Ocean. This would allow them to sail on to spice-rich Asia.

In 1535, the Frenchman Jacques Cartier had sailed inland along the broad St. Lawrence River. Impassable rapids eventually stopped his boats, but during the next century, French adventurers probed the St. Lawrence and Great Lakes region, establishing trading settlements. The rugged French settlers trapped beaver, rabbit, fox, and other animals for their furs; they also traded cheap trinkets with the natives in exchange for furs to send back to Europe.

Samuel de Champlain established one of the

An encounter between Native Americans and a group of Frenchmen in small boats is depicted in this painting entitled "Cartier Discovers the St. Lawrence."

most famous trading posts along the St. Lawrence at Quebec. Champlain befriended two of the region's largest Indian tribes, the Huron and Algonquin. In return, the Indians accepted French missionaries into their settlements. Other Indians were not as friendly. By the mid-1600s, the powerful Iroquois nation was engaged in a bloody war against the French settlements along the St. Lawrence.

Thus occupied in the northeastern part of the continent, the French settlers were still unaware that a mighty river divided the central part of North

America. "Father of Waters" was the English trans-
lation of *missi sippi*, the name the Algonquin Indians
gave the great river that flows south through the
heart of North America.
Undoubtedly, the Indians
named it that because they
knew it was the central river
into which many other
rivers flowed. The Indians
used these rivers to trans-
port trade items such as animal furs and grain.

> **The Mississippi is one of the largest rivers in the world. Waters from more than half of the U.S. states flow into the Mississippi River.**

River life in the frigid North was different from
that in the humid South. For example, northern
Indians made canoes of birch bark. In southern
waters, natives carved dugouts from tree trunks.

Different people with new ways of life . . . all in a
boundless new land for La Salle to investigate.

* * * *

After several dismal weeks on the rolling
Atlantic, La Salle and his companions caught sight
of the North American mainland. Soon they arrived
at the settlement of Montreal, far inland on the St.
Lawrence River. Montreal at that time was farther
west than any other French trading post.

Robert's brother Jean lived in Montreal. He and other priests taught the Indians the language and religion of the French. Montreal seemed very strange to Robert. He was used to stately cathedrals, servants, fine food, and comfortable living. Here he found a very different world with few comforts. The log cabins were small, the food primitive.

Worse than the poor living conditions was the constant threat of danger. French settlers lived in fear of certain Indian tribes. They had made friends with some of the natives, but the Iroquois resented the Europeans. The Iroquois were fierce and deadly foes. They recently had agreed to a peace treaty. Still, in the words of famous historian Francis Parkman, "no man could venture into the forests or the fields without bearing his life in his hands."

Although he came from a rich family, Robert was forced to seek his own fortune. His father had died some years earlier, but because of the vow of poverty he had taken on entering the Jesuit novitiate, he had not been able to accept the inheritance that would normally have been his. Now that he had left the Jesuits, neither his brother Nicholas nor his sister, who together controlled the family funds, was willing to grant him anything more than a small

Settlers in New France faced constant danger from Native Americans, especially members of the Iroquois tribe. This drawing from a 16th-century French book shows an Iroquois scalping a white man. "No Indians of North America ever showed greater ferocity than the Iroquois," one historian has written.

yearly allowance. This meant he needed to find some way to make a living. Robert was only 23 years old, but here in the wild Americas he intended to make something of himself.

Robert had been granted a tract of land for farming at a place along the river near Montreal now known as the La Chine Rapids. But he decided there was a faster, more exciting way than farming to acquire wealth: trading furs with the Indians.

Montreal was the site of a great **rendezvous** each spring. Thousands of Native Americans would converge on the trading settlement, with many animal skins bound up into bales loaded into their large birch-bark canoes. The Indians were experts at catching wild beasts, whose fur hides commanded high prices in Europe. Wealthy men and women were willing to pay almost any price the merchants asked. Many a French frontiersman made his fortune in the American fur trade.

In return, the Indians wanted European cloth and bright *trinkets*–very cheap items, compared to animal furs. They also wanted guns and liquor– products the European settlers in time would wish they'd never provided.

La Salle made his home on a piece of wilderness at the south end of a large river island. He cleared enough trees to build a small fort, and other settlers soon joined him. La Salle charged them rent. He also set up a trading post.

As the owner of a frontier outpost, La Salle paid traders and trappers for their animal pelts. Soon, he had a network of agents obtaining furs from different Indian tribes in different parts of the upper St. Lawrence region. At the same time, he took care to stay on good terms with the natives. He got to know them and learned to communicate with several tribes in their own languages. As he began to explore the woodlands, La Salle ventured many miles into the wild. He yearned to see and learn as much as he could of this vast New France.

La Salle's curiosity about what lay to the west and south increased greatly one winter when he spent some time with a band of Seneca Indians. He was wide-eyed as he listened to them describe another major river, many miles to the south. If he were to travel south along this river far enough, they told him, he eventually would reach the ocean—a different ocean than the Atlantic!

The Indians called this river the Ohio. Historians today are uncertain whether they were speaking of the Ohio River we know or the even greater Mississippi into which it flows—or both. La Salle knew nothing of either waterway.

But news of a river that led to an unnamed ocean was exciting. All the Europeans exploring the Americas in those years hoped to find a direct route through the continent. Perhaps a cargo ship could sail all the way through New France (rather than around it) to the Pacific Ocean and on to the Orient. Might this river be the way through the continent?

La Salle's First Expedition

An Iroquois, wearing a ceremonial mask, peers out of a traditional birch-bark longhouse. On La Salle's first expedition, he and his men had to learn how to live like the natives of the land they were exploring.

2

Restless and eager to explore, La Salle began to plan an expedition. He would need to hire a crew, buy supplies, and obtain trade goods for exchange with the Indians—and all this would cost money. To raise the funds, La Salle sold his frontier property at the end of 1668. Early the next year, La Salle journeyed by canoe to Quebec, the capital of New France, located almost 200 miles down the St. Lawrence toward the Atlantic Ocean. He went to tell the governor of New France about the river he hoped to find and ask for permission to explore along its banks, engage in trade, and ultimately look for a passage to the western sea.

The governor, Daniel de Rémy, Sieur de Courcelles, was happy to approve La Salle's plan. He requested that La Salle join some missionaries, led by two priests, Father Barthélemy and Father François Dollier de Casson, who were about to set off in search of the Mississippi. They had been told of many unknown tribes living along the banks of the great river, and they wished to discover these peoples so they might convert them to Christianity.

La Salle then hired 14 rugged frontiersmen and bought four canoes. He also bought food, guns, gunpowder, and other *provisions*. The small band of missionaries added three more canoes to their river fleet. Some friendly Seneca Indians were chosen to guide the expedition. On July 6, 1669, the group began paddling up the St. Lawrence from Montreal.

The bold French pioneers immediately had to learn to live like Native Americans. They traveled, ate, and sheltered themselves as the Indians did.

Following the Indians' example, the Frenchmen cut cedar strips and fashioned them into frames.

Then they sewed slabs of bark to the frames and filled in small holes with spruce tree sap. These birch-bark canoes were lightweight and thin, but sturdy.

Dollier de Casson, who led the missionaries, was a brave man, a former soldier who was at home in the wild. Another missionary who went along, Father Galinée, later wrote about La Salle's first expedition.

The Indians also bound birch bark over frames to make tents. The travelers adopted this method of shelter as well. Their birch-bark tents protected the French explorers from the elements while they camped.

When they came to dangerous rapids or obstructions in the river, the explorers had to *portage*, or carry their canoes alongside the water through the woods—sometimes for long distances. They paddled for weeks against the strong current of the St. Lawrence. As the miles slipped behind them, the men grew weary. Many became sick. La Salle said very little, but he pulled rhythmically at his paddle, determined to see where the river led.

On August 2, 1669, the tired explorers came upon an amazing sight: a vast body of water like a great sea. It was what is called today Lake Ontario—

the first of the Great Lakes as one journeys westward on the St. Lawrence. Other French adventurers had seen the Great Lakes in the past, but for La Salle and his companions, this was an important moment in their journey. Even more fantastic natural spectacles were in store for them.

For more than a week, they moved along the lower shoreline of the gigantic lake. To their left was wilderness, with no signs of human activity in sight. To the right was gray water extending all the way to the northern horizon.

On one stop, La Salle made friends with some members of the Seneca tribe. Although the Seneca were part of the warring Iroquois nation, these natives were friendly. The Indians who met La Salle invited the travelers to visit their village some miles into the forest. There, the explorers could rest and recover from their illnesses. La Salle hoped the Seneca would provide his expedition with a guide when the journey continued. As the days went

While he stayed with the Seneca, La Salle learned a lot about Indian ways. They taught him how to endure the hardships of the wilderness in all weather, and how to trap and skin wild game and survive off the land.

by, though, the Seneca did not produce a guide.

The Indians had a practical reason not to help the Frenchmen. Because of the Iroquois's dominance of the eastern Great Lakes region, they functioned as middlemen, trading both with the tribes of the interior and with Canadian merchants. If the French had direct access to the Shawnee and other western tribes, the Iroquois would be cut out of the trade chain. They tried to convince the French that it would be foolish to explore further.

However, the French did not understand the Seneca's perspective. Worried that the friendly Indians might become dangerous, La Salle's group resumed their journey. Continuing along, they passed the place where the Niagara River flows into Lake Ontario. They could hear the steady roar of the awesome Niagara Falls a short distance upriver.

Reaching the western shore of Lake Ontario, La Salle's party met another French adventurer named Louis Joliet. Joliet told the missionaries they might make many Christian converts among the Indians living around the other Great Lakes.

La Salle was not interested in exploring the other lakes to the northwest. He wanted to follow a southerly course and search for the fabled water route to the ocean. So the French travelers divided. The missionaries set off to do their work around the other lakes. With the blessings of Father Dollier, La Salle and 13 explorers took some of the supplies and went their own way. La Salle announced that they were returning to Montreal—but once the two groups separated, La Salle told his men they would be searching for the Ohio River instead.

What happened to La Salle's exploration party for the next two years is a mystery. Some historians believe the party found the Ohio River and began paddling downstream. They were forced to stop at the falls of the Ohio, a stretch of powerful rapids near what is today Louisville, Kentucky. And there, La Salle's men apparently deserted him. They must have made their way back to civilization, leaving him alone in the cold, strange wilderness. But La Salle was a capable woodsman. He was able to survive for many months, living off the forest, helped by friendly Indians.

Later, La Salle claimed to have discovered both the Ohio River and the Illinois River. Historians today do not know if this is true. They know only that in 1671 or 1672, La Salle returned to the French settlements along the St. Lawrence.

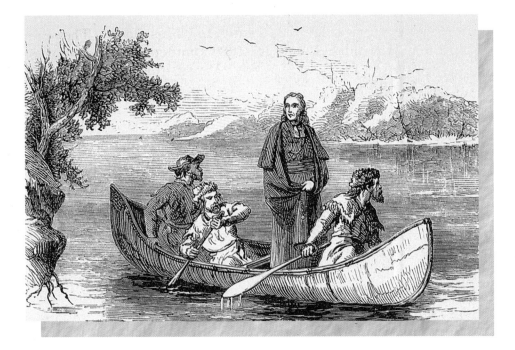

The French missionary Jacques Marquette stands in a canoe paddled by Louis Joliet and others. In 1672 Marquette and Joliet explored the upper Mississippi.

Soon afterward, the fur trader Louis Joliet and a missionary, Father Jacques Marquette, discovered and explored the upper reaches of the Mississippi River. They claimed the great river for France. News of Joliet's findings made La Salle yearn to go exploring once again. Exploring the broad southern section of North America's greatest waterway became La Salle's mission in life.

His years of exploration were only beginning.

Dreams of a
New Empire

A crowd of Indians watch as La Salle's schooner Griffon *is launched into the waters of Lake Erie in August 1679. La Salle built the ship so that he could explore the Great Lakes.*

3

The river discovered by Joliet and Marquette apparently did not lead to the western ocean, but flowed into the Gulf of Mexico some 2,000 miles to the south. That was a very important piece of news. If France could gain control of this gigantic waterway through the heart of North America, the French could build frontier forts at important locations along the big river. France could become the leading European power in the Americas.

Supported by forts along the great central river, the French could protect their traders from enemies. Backed by this military power, French traders and trappers could win the lion's share of the fur trade throughout the interior of America. That would help France's economy at home—and it would make many French traders extremely rich.

Meanwhile, such a strong presence all along the frontier, from the Gulf of Mexico to the far north, would serve an even greater purpose: It would block explorers and settlers from England—France's long-time rival—from expanding westward. If France controlled the Mississippi, eventually most or all of the continent could belong to France!

La Salle believed he should be a leader in helping France take advantage of this opportunity. And why should he not take the lead? After all, he was an experienced woodsman and explorer, and he had earned the respect of the French settlers and Indians along the St. Lawrence.

The new governor of New France shared La Salle's ambitions. His name was Louis de Buade, Comte de Frontenac, and he was a skillful governor. When the troublesome Iroquois once more threatened the French fur trade, Frontenac raised a large army of Frenchmen and Huron Indians, enemies of the Iroquois. But rather than fight, Frontenac invited all the natives to sit down to a *peace parley*. The Iroquois were persuaded to let the French expand peacefully around the region of Lake Ontario–at least for the time being. Soon, a stone fort was built on Lake Ontario to protect French fur traders in that region. It was named Fort Frontenac.

Unfortunately, construction of the fort had not received approval from the king. Governor Frontenac soon found himself in trouble. La Salle agreed to return home to resolve the situation. With the governor's blessings, in late 1674 La Salle took a ship back to France. Frontenac, writing to the king, said his friend La Salle was "more capable than anybody else I know here to accomplish every kind of enterprise and discovery."

At the fabulous French palace of Versailles, La Salle made friends with one of the king's most important officials, Jean Baptiste Colbert. Colbert liked La Salle's plan to expand French power in New France. He encouraged King Louis to help the brave explorer.

La Salle impressed others in France, too. They found La Salle to be a man of few words–but when

Jean Baptiste Colbert was one of King Louis XIV's trusted advisors. Colbert liked La Salle and urged the king to support his plans to explore the Mississippi River.

he spoke, others were wise to listen to him. One acquaintance wrote in a journal, "I have never heard anybody speak whose words carried with them more marks of truth."

La Salle obtained from King Louis XIV a land grant for Fort Frontenac and the surrounding forests. The king also granted him control of fur trading in the region for five years and agreed to an arrangement for maintaining the fort's army garrison with profits from the fur trade. La Salle still had to borrow money to help finance his expeditions, but the king's approval was very important.

La Salle returned to the frontier. He strength-ened his fort and soon was the most powerful Frenchman along the upper St. Lawrence River. This made him disliked by many French settlers, including rival fur traders. He also angered Jesuit missionaries in the region, because he befriended other missionaries.

His enemies were worried about La Salle's grow-ing power. They did not understand that power and fame on the St. Lawrence were not what he wanted. La Salle was interested in exploring this great land.

He ordered the building of a formidable five-gun ship, the *Griffon* (spelled *Griffin* in some history books). This **schooner** would become his private ves-sel for exploring the Great Lakes. These are large freshwater bodies of water. Sailing on the Great Lakes can be challenging and dangerous–as many shipwrecks on the lakes have demonstrated, even in modern times.

La Salle remained in charge of Fort Frontenac for several years. During that time, he prepared for his next major expedition. In August 1679, with his crew firing a farewell cannonball and singing a hymn, La Salle directed the *Griffon* into the open water of Lake Erie.

Claiming the
Mississippi
for France

A reconstructed French fort on one bank of the Mississippi River. La Salle dreamed that one day he would establish a network of French forts along the mighty river. These would offer protection to French traders in North America, and enable France to control the entire continent.

4

*T*he *Griffon* sliced through the cold waters of the Great Lakes. When La Salle came to the western end of Lake Erie, he made his way up through Lake St. Clair to Lake Huron. He passed northward along the eastern shore of the present-day state of Michigan. Then he entered Lake Michigan and sailed down to its southern tip.

To the Indians, the *Griffon* looked like an incredible floating fort. When it anchored in a cove near the trading post St. Ignace, they crowded their canoes alongside to stare at it more closely.

La Salle sailed the *Griffon* across Lake Huron, stopping several times to trade for furs. When the ship reached the lower tip of Lake Michigan, he took some of his men ashore and sent the *Griffon* home. He wanted the *Griffon* to take the furs back to the French settlements and then come back for him with supplies to build another ship. La Salle planned to use this second vessel to explore both the Illinois River and the Mississippi River.

The *Griffon* never arrived at the French settlements. Perhaps it was lost in one of the lakes' notorious autumn gales. Or the crew may have stolen the furs, deliberately sunk the ship, and divided the spoils; or hostile natives may have wiped them out.

Meanwhile, La Salle and the others began probing the wilderness on foot, treading into what is today the state of Illinois.

Accompanying La Salle were several individuals whose names would also be remembered in the chronicles of French exploration. One was Father Louis Hennepin, a Franciscan missionary. Hennepin, by many accounts, was as eager to explore unknown lands and acquire wealth and glory as he

La Salle had befriended Father Louis Hennepin and brought him to the New World in 1677. The priest was fascinated by exploration. He would later write a book about La Salle's adventures in the Mississippi River valley.

was to convert the Indians. The other man would prove to be La Salle's most trusted friend: Henri de Tonty. This Italian soldier had been introduced to La Salle in France. Tonty had lost a hand while fighting in the French army, but he knew how to use his artificial hand, made of iron, very effectively as both a weapon and tool. As a result, he had earned the nickname "Iron Hand."

Tonty had told La Salle he wished to accompany him on his next expedition, and La Salle had agreed. In New France, Tonty had immediately proved his worth. He was the one who had supervised unruly Indians and Frenchmen while they built the *Griffon*. Despite his artificial hand, Tonty was a capable lieutenant. He sometimes helped La Salle overcome seemingly impossible odds.

A third member of the expedition would also become a valuable ally in the coming years. This was a Shawnee Indian named Nika. Not only was Nika a wonderful guide who knew the lakes and rivers; he also was an excellent hunter who provided the hungry Frenchmen with wild game.

La Salle's party built another frontier outpost, Fort Crevecoeur ("Fort Heartbreak" in English). This was on the Illinois River. The travelers waited there during the winter for the other explorers to return with much-needed supplies. When the relief never came, La Salle decided in March 1680 to make his way back to the settlements for help.

Montreal was a thousand miles to the east. La Salle was never one to avoid hardship, however. He left Tonty in command of the fort and set forth, accompanied by Nika and several disgruntled Frenchmen. At first they tried to travel by canoe, but the water was too icy, so they soon found themselves trekking overland through the bitter winter. They were constantly cold, wet, and nearly starved. They had to make detours and sometimes cover their trail in order to avoid hostile Iroquois warriors.

La Salle took more than two months to reach the warmth of Fort Frontenac.

Back on the Illinois River, the French and their Indian friends were starving and weary of the expedition. While La Salle was gone, there was a *mutiny* at Fort Crevecoeur. Tonty had to flee for his life.

When La Salle returned and discovered what had happened, he chased down the rebels and had them taken in chains back to Governor Frontenac to face justice. Tonty was rescued, but the Iroquois massacred many of La Salle's Indian friends.

During this time Father Hennepin had undergone a frightening ordeal of his own. La Salle had dispatched him and two other men to paddle down the Illinois–if possible, to find the headwaters of the Mississippi. They were to seek a different tribe of Indians who reportedly lived further west: the Sioux.

When Hennepin found the Sioux, they took him captive! After a time, Daniel Greysolon, Sieur Dulhut rescued Hennepin.

> Hennepin later wrote that when he was with the Sioux, he came across the place where the Mississippi starts, and that he journeyed many miles down the great river. Historians doubt these claims, however.

*La Salle and his followers enter the Mississippi in this
painting by George Catlin.*

Dulhut (also spelled Duluth) was another French explorer who became famous for his investigations around Lake Superior.

Meanwhile, La Salle suffered more hardships on this disastrous expedition than he ever could have imagined. He was hungry and cold, and at one point he temporarily went blind. The betrayals of his followers may have upset him the most, though.

When La Salle at last returned to the French settlements in the north, he had to get his affairs in order before he could think about exploring the Mississippi River valley. And his affairs were a mess! He had borrowed money for supplies, and now he was unable to repay his creditors with furs. They were angry with him, but the governor offered him important help. The governor showed La Salle how to manage his business carefully and how to arrange for repaying his debts. Soon, La Salle was able to obtain loans for a new expedition.

This adventure—which was to become his most famous—began in September 1681 on Lake Ontario. La Salle commanded about 30 French woodsmen and 100 Native Americans. His faithful friend Tonty once more was his second in command.

By December, he and his party were making their way down the Illinois River. Many of the Indians had deserted him by this time because of the hard conditions and the coming winter. The river was already frozen, so his men had to pull their birch-bark canoes across ice. They did not stop. In early February 1682, their canoes knifed into the wide waters of the Mississippi. By now, La Salle's party included 23 Frenchmen and 31 Indians.

La Salle had two objectives: first, to navigate the full length of the Mississippi, which had never been explored extensively by Europeans; and second, to construct French forts at strategic places along the river, giving his country a great advantage in the quest for control of America.

One of these new fortresses was Fort Prudhomme. La Salle named it in honor of one of his trusted men, gunsmith Pierre Prudhomme. While they were building the structure, Prudhomme went off into the wilderness to explore and did not return for many days. The others feared Indians had captured him. When he finally made his way back to the fort, he admitted he had merely gotten lost. This problem was all too common for Europeans on the frontier. La Salle was not angry. Instead, he was so glad to see his friend again that he put Prudhomme in charge of the fort when he headed downstream.

La Salle made friends with the Indian tribes they met as they paddled southward on the wide, smooth river. To prove their friendship, the Native Americans smoked *peace pipes* with the Europeans. These pipes were lengths of hollow wood, carved and painted, usually adorned with colorful bird feathers.

The Indians on the lower Mississippi lived differently than the Native Americans in the north. Their villages and houses were made of straw and mud, unlike the Indian homes around the Great Lakes. The land here was also very different from what the French were used to in the north. It was flat and covered with pine forests. Near the coast were swamps with miles of cypress trees and stumps rising from shallow water. The explorers encountered frightening alligators, creatures unknown in northern waters. Compared to the upper Mississippi and the Great Lakes, the weather was warm.

On April 6, the great river divided into three channels. With much excitement, the travelers realized that the water was becoming salty. Soon, they reached the very mouth of the Mississippi. La Salle's party had paddled all the way from the frozen north to the warm Gulf of Mexico!

Two days later, several miles inland from the gulf, La Salle staged a formal ceremony. He claimed the Mississippi River basin for France and named it Louisiana for King Louis XIV. The men planted a French flag, raised a cross, and praised God.

Although the news would not reach the European colonies for many weeks to come, this was one of the most glorious days in French history. La Salle had secured the whole length of the western frontier of North America for his country.

A painting of the French king Louis XIV on horseback. In 1684 La Salle convinced King Louis that he could create a permanent French colony at the mouth of the Mississippi River.

The Hard Journey Home 5

La Salle had achieved his dream. Now he faced a new challenge: getting home alive.

This was not so easy. The party now had to move upstream. And soon, near Chickasaw Bluffs, La Salle fell deathly ill. He had to be taken ashore and put to bed in a crude stockade his men had built on the trip downriver. He was near death, unable to travel, for six weeks.

While La Salle lay sick, he sent Tonty ahead to report their claim of the Mississippi River basin. The news must have electrified the French settlers. Leaders like Governor Frontenac were jubilant. But not all the French rejoiced in the explorer's success. La Salle had many enemies—notably traders who had long felt La Salle had become too powerful. They resented his interference in their private operations.

La Salle began to recover in July. He now could travel again, but only a little way at a time. Not until September did he manage to travel up the Illinois River to Michilimackinac, a mission outpost and trading center near the place where Lakes Huron, Michigan, and Superior come together.

Because La Salle could not travel fast, he was afraid to continue on to Montreal and Quebec. He knew winter storms could hit before they arrived. Rather than risk being caught on the freezing lakes and rivers, he decided to spend the winter downriver at a place called Starved Rock. This was a high bluff near the place where the Kankakee River enters the Illinois.

Tonty had rejoined the expedition, and he and La Salle focused on building a new fort at Starved Rock. They oversaw the building of lodgings for the men and storage houses, all protected by a wall on three sides and a high, rocky cliff overlooking the river on the fourth. They called it Fort St. Louis. Hundreds of Native Americans were camped near

Fort St. Louis. From several different tribes, they all respected the hardy French leader. Many of them looked to him for protection against the Iroquois.

> La Salle's Fort St. Louis was located several hundred miles north of the modern-day city of Saint Louis, Missouri.

But La Salle was not happy to be spending the winter there. Now that he had navigated down the Mississippi, he knew France could keep control of the river only if he and his countrymen built more forts and established reliable communications between them. He wanted to build a large fort near the river's mouth at the Gulf of Mexico; he wanted to return to France to discuss these matters at the royal court; and he was impatient to put all his plans into action. He did not want to wait until spring.

His anxiety increased when word came that Frontenac was no longer governor of New France. The new governor, Le Fèbvre de La Barre, was an enemy of Frontenac—and, as a result, he was La Salle's enemy as well. Frontenac had been La Salle's friend and supporter, but he was not well liked by other merchants or by some of the mission leaders. When La Salle returned to Montreal, he knew he

This map, drawn in 1684 by a man who explored
with La Salle, shows the two forts he established on the
Illinois River, Fort St. Louis and Fort Crevecoeur.

would find himself out of favor with the new
government—despite his marvelous, hard-earned
achievement on the Mississippi.

When spring came and he finally reached home,
La Salle saw that things were even worse than he

had feared. La Barre had taken possession of La Salle's Fort Frontenac, had ordered its furs and other merchandise to be sold, and had taken much of the profit for himself. Still worse, he was sending one of his men down the Illinois to take over La Salle's new outpost, Fort St. Louis.

By a twist of politics, the conqueror of the mighty Mississippi had been rewarded with the loss of almost everything he owned. There was only one thing for La Salle to do: go to France and appeal directly to the king.

In 1684, La Salle once more crossed the Atlantic to France. This was an uncertain period in his life, and as he made the voyage, he probably felt angry and defeated. Only King Louis could right the wrongs committed against him by Governor La Barre. In Paris, the downcast explorer's spirits must have soared when the king agreed to see him.

In order to make his proposal more attractive, La Salle presented the king with a map that distorted the true path of the Mississippi. As later events would clearly demonstrate, La Salle himself was probably not certain about the exact location of the Mississippi's mouth, so he may have simply decided to go with a map that would best further his own interests. His map made the river seem to veer west, so that its mouth was on the western coast of the Gulf of Mexico, in present-day Texas. This would have been an ideal spot from which to harass the Spanish and raid their silver mines.

La Salle further led the king to believe that the French would be aided in their efforts against the Spanish by the **Algonquian confederacy**, which he had attempted to build in the Illinois River valley years before. He told Louis and his ministers that this confederacy now numbered 15,000 strong, although this was certainly not the case.

After hearing all this, the king agreed to restore Fort Frontenac and Fort St. Louis to La Salle's authority. He even appointed La Salle governor of the new Louisiana territory. King Louis also liked La Salle's idea of building a major fort at the mouth of the Mississippi River. Placed at a commanding location on the Gulf of Mexico, it would be a vital addition to France's defenses in the New World.

The king had another assignment for La Salle as well. King Louis was keenly interested in obtaining from the Americas a form of riches more valuable than furs—he wanted a share of the gold and silver the Spanish were bringing home from Mexico. Now that his man La Salle was going to establish a foothold on the gulf, the king assumed La Salle could simply lead an expedition from there into northern Mexico to take over Spanish silver mines.

La Salle had hoped to be given a single ship and a handpicked band of eager explorers to help him build up France's military muscle along the Mississippi. Instead, King Louis dispatched four ships. Four hundred people, including almost 200 men and women who wished to settle in the lower Mississippi River valley, were crowded aboard.

This was not exactly what La Salle had had in mind for his next expedition. He was thankful to be in the king's good graces, though. So in summer 1684, he set forth with his small fleet, bound directly for the Gulf of Mexico.

Shortly before leaving France, he wrote a farewell letter to his mother. "We all have good hope of a happy success," he reported cheerfully.

But it was not to be.

The Last
Expedition

La Salle's men land at Matagorda Bay, on the Gulf Coast of present-day Texas, on February 20, 1685. La Salle was unsure exactly how to find the mouth of the Mississippi River from the sea. He missed it by more than 400 miles. This was the first of a series of problems that would plague La Salle's attempt at building a colony.

6

It was a miserable voyage. Many of the passengers and soldiers became sick. La Salle and the commander of the ships argued. In the Caribbean, Spanish pirates attacked them, capturing one of their cargo ships—a crippling blow to the would-be colonists. To make matters worse, La Salle became very sick and had to be taken ashore. Weeks passed before he was well enough to return to sea. During that time, some of his men ran away.

When they entered the Gulf of Mexico, La Salle found himself facing another crisis. Finding the mouth of the Mississippi by sailing all the way down it was one thing. Finding it again from the open sea was quite a different matter. They had no reliable charts or maps by which to navigate. They ended up sailing 400 miles past the river's entrance. In early 1685, La Salle landed on the coast of what today is Texas. He sent patrols to find the great river, but the Frenchmen were too far off course.

La Salle decided to make the best of a bad start by building the colony at Matagorda Bay. But before they could settle ashore, disaster struck. Their supply ship, *L'Aimable*, sank in the bay. The ship carried most of the colonists' food and belongings.

Soon the escort ship *Joly* had to go back to France. Later, a drunken pilot wrecked the other ship, *La Belle*. Now, La Salle had no way to explore the gulf by sea, and the colonists were cut off from their homeland.

The settlers fell into despair. But they managed to drag enough wood from the inland forests through the marsh to build a small fortress on the bay. They gave it the same name as La Salle's earlier settlement on the Illinois River: Fort St. Louis.

La Salle realized, however, that they could not survive as a colony on this unfriendly coast, isolated from established French trade routes. He believed that their only hope lay in finding the Mississippi and moving the colony there. That way La Salle's colony could communicate with the French forts upriver and begin to spread French influence throughout the Mississippi River valley.

In April 1686, he set off with a small body of men to investigate the land to the northeast. They roamed for months and met different tribes of Native Americans. When they came to one of the large rivers of southern Texas, La Salle believed it must be the Mississippi. Perhaps he let himself fall victim to wishful thinking–or perhaps he realized the error but was afraid to tell his disgruntled men this was not the river they sought.

They built a small fort on the riverbank. Then La Salle and his main force turned back to the settlement at Matagorda Bay. They left several men to maintain the new outpost. These soldiers were never heard from again.

In January 1687 La Salle explained to his few remaining followers at Matagorda Bay that if they were to survive he must lead some of the men up

This detail from a 17th-century French map of
Louisiana inaccurately shows the Mississippi River
flowing much farther to the west than it actually does.

the Mississippi and Illinois Rivers, all the way to the established French settlements. Hopefully, they would reach the St. Lawrence by spring, and then they could return in summer.

The journey was bound to be difficult. They were low on supplies, including gunpowder for their muskets. They would need the help of Indian guides—and they had no trinkets left with which to attract the natives. The men were dressed in rags, some wearing shreds of their doomed ships' sails.

La Salle and 16 men left the fort and trudged northward across the marsh and prairie. A few of these men could be counted on to support him to the end. They included his brother Jean and two nephews. La Salle also had some enemies in his party. Among them were two men named Liotot and Duhaut, who had come to hate their leader.

After two months of slow progress, some of the men went hunting and managed to kill two buffalo. The hunters, who included Liotot and Duhaut, set up camp to skin the beasts. They sent word for the main party to send horses to carry the meat. La Salle dispatched his nephew, Moranget Cavelier, and another man to bring the horses to the hunters.

The night before they planned to return to La Salle with the much-needed buffalo meat, Liotot and Duhaut conspired with the others to murder Moranget and two other men loyal to La Salle. They killed the three sleeping men with an axe.

When no one returned to the main camp the next day, March 19, 1687, La Salle became worried. He set off himself to learn what was wrong, taking with him a priest named Father Anastus Douay.

As they walked, the missionary wrote later, La Salle seemed strangely preoccupied with talk of God and of how the Lord had preserved him from so many dangers during his many years of adventure. The priest wrote, "I saw him overwhelmed with a profound sense of sadness. . . . He was so much moved that I scarcely knew him."

Perhaps La Salle knew his time had come to die.

As they approached the hunters' camp on the banks of a stream, one of the conspirators came forward to talk to La Salle. He lured the leader into an ambush where Liotot and Duhaut were hidden, guns ready. When La Salle was within range, the plotters shot him in the head. Then they stripped his corpse and left him lying in the tall prairie grass.

And so one of France's bravest and most ambitious explorers died—not from the natural dangers he faced so often, or by the hand of hostile Indians, but from a French musket ball.

* * * *

Sieur de La Salle was a true pathfinder. He spent his life in America battling treacherous river currents, plodding through waist-deep snow, and enduring countless other frontier hardships. La Salle never married; he probably knew he would never be content with a settled home life.

He was much more than an adventurer, however. He navigated the Mississippi River all the way to the Gulf of Mexico—an epic achievement that

La Salle remains a hero of French exploration. This large statue of him stands in Luneville, France.

required wise planning and endless perseverance. In the process, he established outposts that would serve his country well as the American frontier expanded.

These forts also became gathering points for different Indian tribes. La Salle had made friends with many of the natives. These alliances would help France control the midwestern region of North America into the next century.

After La Salle's death, his murderers went to live with an Indian tribe in Texas, taking La Salle's remaining relatives as prisoners. But they soon quarreled among themselves, and Liotot and Duhaut were shot in much the same way they had killed La Salle. The explorer's brother and nephew, with a few others, eventually made their way up the Mississippi to the St. Lawrence and on to France, where they told their tragic story.

The ragtag colony at Matagorda Bay, as La Salle had feared, did not survive long. When a band of Spanish *conquistadors* found it, the fortress was deserted. The Spaniards learned that natives had captured it, probably killing the colonists.

And what became of the loyal lieutenant, Henri de Tonty? He was not with La Salle on the disastrous final expedition. When he learned of La Salle's death, Tonty struggled through the wilds to reach Matagorda Bay to see if he could help the colonists. He found only Indians on the Texas coastal plain.

For another 15 years, Tonty continued to be a leader among French explorers and traders from the Great Lakes to the lower Mississippi River. He is believed to have died near modern-day Mobile, Alabama. To the end, Tonty shared the vision of his longtime commander and friend: to make France the ruler of the North American frontier.

Chronology

1643 La Salle is born at Rouen, France, on November 22.

1667 La Salle arrives in Montreal in the New World.

1669 La Salle begins three years of exploring the St. Lawrence River, along Lake Ontario, and southward into the wilderness.

1679 Sets out to explore the Great Lakes and Illinois River.

1680 Expedition into the Great Lakes and Illinois River ends in disaster.

1681 La Salle begins his famous expedition southward to the mouth of the Mississippi.

1682 On April 9, two days after reaching the Gulf of Mexico, La Salle formally declares the Mississippi River basin to be French territory, naming it Louisiana.

1684 La Salle's expedition to colonize the mouth of the Mississippi sails from France with the king's blessings.

1685 After a long, disastrous voyage, La Salle's party lands on the coast of modern-day Texas.

1687 La Salle and a small band of men set out by land to try to make their way to the French settlements on the Mississippi for help; on March 19, La Salle is assassinated by several of his own men.

1803 The United States acquires La Salle's territory from France in the Louisiana Purchase.

Glossary

Algonquian confederacy–an alliance of Native American tribes along the Mississippi River that agreed to live in peace with the French.

conquistadors–Spanish leaders in the conquest of the Americas.

Great Lakes–five connected freshwater lakes bordering the United States and Canada, including Lakes Superior, Huron, Michigan, Erie, and Ontario.

Jesuits–the Roman Catholic Society of Jesus, a religious order founded by St. Ignatius Loyola in 1534 and devoted to missionary and education work.

Louisiana–large area of land known as the Mississippi River basin, claimed for France by La Salle in 1682, and named in honor of the French king, Louis XIV.

missionary–a person who tries to convert other people to his or her religion.

mutiny–a revolt against discipline or against a commanding officer.

navigation–the science of directing the course of a seagoing vessel, and of determining its position.

notary–a public official who certifies documents or deeds to make them official.

peace parley–a peace conference with an enemy for discussion of points in dispute.

peace pipe–an American Indian ceremonial pipe carved from hollow wood, usually painted and adorned with colorful bird feathers.

portage–Indian term referring to the act of carrying canoes and small boats over land, to avoid rapids and falls in order to reach smooth waters.

provisions–a stock of food and water.

rendezvous–a meeting or gathering. A rendezvous was held each spring in Montreal and drew thousands of Native Americans to the trading settlement, along with their abundance of furs. Many French frontiersmen became very wealthy there, since these furs commanded such high prices in Europe.

schooner–a small sailing vessel, usually with two masts.

trinkets–small ornaments or items of little value that explorers carried to trade with natives they encountered.

Further Reading

Coulter, Tony. *La Salle and the Explorers of the Mississippi.* New York: Chelsea House Publishers, 1991.

Foster, William C., ed. *The La Salle Expedition to Texas: The Journal of Henri Joutel.* Austin: Texas State Historical Association, 1998.

Gallagher, Jim. *Hernando de Soto and the Exploration of Florida.* Philadelphia: Chelsea House Publishers, 2000.

Hargrove, Jim. *The World's Great Explorers: René-Robert Cavelier, Sieur de La Salle.* Chicago: Children's Press, 1990.

Harmon, Daniel E. *Jacques Cartier and the Exploration of Canada.* Philadelphia: Chelsea House Publishers, 2001.

Law, Kevin. *Canada.* Philadelphia: Chelsea House Publishers, 1999.

Parkman, Francis. *La Salle and the Discovery of the Great West* [1869]. Williamstown, Mass.: Corner House Publishers, 1968 [reprint edition].

Syme, Ronald. *La Salle of the Mississippi.* New York: William Morrow & Company, 1953.

Picture Credits

DANIEL E. HARMON is an editor and writer living in Spartanburg, South Carolina. He has written several books on humor and history, and has contributed historical and cultural articles to the *New York Times, Music Journal, Nautilus,* and many other periodicals. He is the managing editor of *Sandlapper: The Magazine of South Carolina* and is editor of *The Lawyer's PC* newsletter. His books include *Civil War Leaders* and *Fighting Units of the American War of Independence.*